APULIA

*The publishers wish to thank
the Tourist Board of the Apulia Region
for the valuable collaboration
in the realization of the present volume*

APULIA

photographs by
MARIO DE BIASI

texts by
GUIDO GEROSA

english version by
PETER LAURITZEN

MAGNUS

APULIA, LAND OF MISTERY

Apulia, noblest of the southern regions. Thus the Romans called Caesar Augustus' II Region, the most variegated of the lands of south eastern Italy. Bathed by the Adriatic, made of sea, forest, rocks, hills and green deserts. Inhabited by the Apuli or the Iapygians; subdivided into Messapia in the South, Peucezi in the centre and Dauni to the north of the actual province of Foggia. The Salentine peninsula, inhabited in the Roman era by the Messapian peoples, was called Calabria, a term that only in the seventh century passed with the Byzantine domination to indicate that other great peninsula of southern Italy. Over the span of millennia people from remote districts came down into Apulia. But when Greek colonists emigrated there, the region became a bridgehead to the Balkan peninsula and the world of the East: a role that it has never lost. The Via Appia ended at Brindisi, the principal port for traffic with the Orient. This was the most important artery of communication between Greece and Rome. It also continued North with the immense network of roads laid out by the Romans as a symbol of their civilization and ended at Hadrian's Wall in today's Scotland.

Later with the Crusades, and up until the reign of Frederick II, Apulia consolidated its fame as a bridge between the West and Greece, Constantinople and the Holy Land. It developed into a region of encounters, of exchange and of commerce.

Treasures arrived from the sea to this miserly land and the only reality in which these were reflected was in the splendour of its cathedrals. However there is a great paradox perpetuated in Apulian history. Apulia is the most typically Mediterranean civilization. It has housed the Italic and Messapic world. It has opened itself to Pythagorian, Illyrian, Hellenistic influence and has also attracted Greeks, Normans, Swabians, Saracens and the Crusaders who established bases here for their great assault on the Holy Land. But Apulia has remained curiously isolated from the picturesque South of the great literary tradition.

When the famous foreign travellers of the eighteenth and nineteenth century visited Campania, Sicily and the Abruzzi, oddly enough they left Apulia out of their itineraries. Only archaeologists like Lenormant and Keppel went there. But they were less interested in the enchantments of the landscape than in the bitterness of the life there. They were impressed by the droughts, by the malarial swamps, by the abandonment of the fields and by the skeletal thinness of the inhabitants. Lenormant wrote in 1866: « The monotony of the Great Apulian Plain is not even redeemed by the prospect of the mountains that enclose it on either side. Only in the winter months it is used by the innumerable flocks that descend to the plain. For the rest of the year it remains a desert in which one cannot find a living thing. The soil is extremely fertile and could become the granary of all Italy or a garden of vines like the land of Bari which borders it on the south east. Instead... ».

Instead dryness and misery reigned. But through one of history's ironies, it was in this land, so miserly in resources that in time there developed remarkable legends and spirituality.

That Apulia is one of the realms of the spirit is demonstrated by the majestic silence of its cathedrals. Great Romanesque cathedrals rise up at Troia, Bitonto, Canosa, Trani, Bisceglie, Molfetta, Altamura, Bitetto and Andria. In Bari there is the splendid Basilica of St. Nicholas where the throne of the Bishop Elia is a work of the finest Romanesque sculpture, not only in Apulia. I do not know if one has reflected enough on the austere solemnity of this region, charged to an unbelieveable degree with monuments. The rocky, stoney presence of a solemn and enigmatic poetry deserves a place to itself in the world of Byzantine and Romanesque art.

The religiousness of Apulia is something profoundly rooted in the spirit of this land. It is notably different from any other manifestation of Southern piety. There is a true and proper religious itinerary in the Gargano for whoever is anxious to listen to the voices of the spirits. The memory of Padre Pio of Pietralcina is alive at San Giovanni Rotondo. One can revive moments of the teaching and profund influence that this friar exercised on the life of the people. It is still evident in the endless pilgrimages to his *Casa di Sollievo della Sofferenza*, the house for the relief of suffering. Another stage on this spiritual itinerary is Monte Sant'Angelo, the famous sanctuary that attracts crowds of the

faithful. Even St. Francis wanted to come here to pray. The Archangel appeared there in a grotto in 490. And there where he touched the earth, the Longobards constructed a sanctuary. Here the Crusaders came to have their arms consacrated before embarking for the Holy Land. Nor did they neglect to stop at the Basilica of Santa Maria Maggiore at Siponto, one of the most beautiful jewels of Apulian Romanesque, rising above the remains of a buried city.
The pilgrims advanced along the Via Sacra penetrating into the heart of the Gargano. Amid fields of sunflowers they arrived at the beautiful church of San Leonardo at Siponto, majestic with its superb entrance carved with tales of the battles fought for the faith. The itinerary concludes with the church of Santa Maria di Siponto near Manfredonia. Even in our own days this Apulian itinerary inspires a profound reconsideration of the reasons of the faith.
To this is added the inimitable suggestiveness of the religious festivities. A caleidoscope of processions and sacred representations that evoke ancient miraculous appearances, of pilgimages and of prayers by the sea.
Holy Week in Taranto is outstanding among all these with its famous processions of the *Addolorata* and the Mysteries that animate Maundy Thursday and Good Friday.
The faithful advance at the slow rythm of a cadenced pace marked by the swaying motion of the « trucculande » and the « perdune ».
The procession of the Trees at Manduria is just as evocative. The devout who follow the

painting of San Pietro in Bevagno bear on their shoulders a mass of thick branches of wild plants. And thus one has the impression that an entire thick forest moves and walks, exactly as in final nightmare in *Macbeth*.
The procession of Corpus Domini at Polignano a Mare is also extremely beautiful.
The confraternities parade slowly, with vestments and beautiful fantastic costumes. The men bear religious emblems along with the sorrowful statue of Christ. And finally crying emotionally, they crowd around the sumptuous altar set up in the Piazza del Duomo and around the pavillion from where the Benediction is given. Catholic religiousness here often passed into pagan usage and was transformed into ritual magic. This land is a land of mystery: a secret and inaccessible Italy, the dark realm of the profound.
Thus there are the rhythms of the sorcerers and the witchs and the strange and disturbing dances of the *tarantolati*. Esoteric religious practises are lost in the night of time. This region is permeated with millenary history. There is archaic evidence of the Neolithic in the cromlechs, the menhir stones and the speculae at Palombara and Zinzulusa; the grotto of the Devil at Santa Maria di Leuca and the necropoli of Calenella.
Extremely ancient rites and uses are knit together with folklore ceremonies, with historical memories and with the testimony of Christian faith. A characteristic carnival is celebrated at Massafra with beautiful allegorical floats. On the third Sunday in

September Saracen raids are evoked in the Palio della Mezzaluna which takes place in the agricultural centre of the Ionian Murgia, a town built on the two shores of the Gravina di San Marco. And during the festival of the Holy Doctors, the airy « Cavalcade of the Angels » is traditional.
One cannot understand Apulia without reflecting on this singular mixture of devotion and superstition, on this fiery marriage of mystic paganism and faith.
The other characteristic of Apulia that leaves one astonished is the extreme clarity of its landscape: a series of boundless paintings. The perfect furrows, the limpid geometry of the rows, the ordered series of farms on the Great Apulian Plain and the interminable grey stain of the olives on the Salentine plain. And then the rich pallette of the seascapes: tall cliffs that plunge into the foam, white houses positioned in a fabulous scenery of dunes, splashes of light and an intense blue that contrasts with colours more vivid than those of the sky. An intense, unreal glow stands out on all this scene, violently illuminating the landscape. « An irritating clarity that is fed by an abundance of limestone » (Giuseppe Cassieri).
It could be said that stone in Apulia lives in its dazzling whiteness, a burning white like that of the marble of Trani and Apicena and of the soft stone in the surroundings of Lecce. Perhaps it is these archaic qualities, the survival of ancient traditions and evocations, that have preserved Apulia intact for us. Even the great currents of consumerism and

mass tourism that have bent the better part of the South to their requirements, have not succeeded in ruining it. Today the wakening of Apulia promises great developments. There is a revolution underway in agriculture, in industry, in communications and in commerce. But even this activity has not interfered with a beauty so jealous of its solitude.

Closed up in the cult of its own rigorous splendour, Apulia is nonetheless anything but a remote, aestheticizing Arcadia. Instead it is a land of lively, pragmatic energies with a clear predominance of historic, sociological and political interests over those of pure fantasy. The finest scholars, leaders, combattants and ideologists of the Southern question have come from here: Gaetano Salvemini, Giuseppe Di Vittorio and Tommaso Fiore. When the first battles were fought in Italy for the emancipation of the manual labourer, the signal for the insurrection of the working classes came from Cerignola, Andria, Canosa and Sannicandro. From Maglie came Aldo Moro, a politician of a tragic destiny, whose influence on the recent history of Italy is being increasingly appreciated. And here a century ago, a typographer-editor-book seller from Bari laid the foundations of Laterza, that glorious publishing house that has had such a role in the cultural history and in the civic committments of our country and in its union with the philosopher Benedetto Croce, awakened our Italian accademic world and made it less provincial.

Beauty in the landscape, profundity in culture, adventurous contacts with the East: these are the moments of Apulia's vital presence. Apulia is difficult to describe as a unit because it possesses so many different characteristics that have made it an assembly of worlds. Examining only the principal ones, there are many Apulias.

From the mountains of Daunia to the extreme south west, green valleys open wide to the Great Apulian Plain.

A succession of solid villages is marshalled on the heights.

The intimacy of mountainous Italy breathes a whiff of Adriatic air. Remote echoes arrive from the East and from Ionian civilization. These lands present the bitter and wizened face of Apulia, gaunt and saddened by the decadence in both men and things, but also ennobled by the great Mediterranean light that illuminates reality.

Troia, long dried up and troubled, is set out along the ridge of a range with steep sides. It was the recent home of Antonio Salandra, the Prime Minister during Italy's intervention in the First World War. It has lived through long periods of decadence, but still conserves the noble qualities of the Dauni and the Apulian peoples who founded it and of Robert Guiscard who conquered it. The grandiose cathedral has all the fascination of Tyrrenhian art with spectacular accents in the façade and apses.

Going north toward the landscapes of the Great Plain, one encounters the proud «Lucera of the Saracens» which dominates the Capitanata. The laments of King Enzo from his prison in Bologna still echo in these lands of silence: «And go to the flat Apulia – the great Catapana – where day and night you find my heart». Frederick II resided for a long time at Lucera, building a powerfully armed fortress and assigning it to the Saracens of the Mazzara Valley. They gave a great impetus to the city, transforming it into a forest of mosques and minarets. The intolerance of the Angevins drove them away and it is only with recent excavations that proof has emerged of the great massacre that effaced them from the region that they had embaellished. The nobility of Lucera is evident in the fortress of Carlo d'Anjou, in the majestic Cathedral of the Assunta, in the fourteenth century church of San Francesco and in many palaces. An ancient history is stratified in the old buildings of the Capitanata. This was the land of the great transmigrations of human and animal movement: the Apenines' grazing animals descended along its sheep tracks. Controlling this traffic led to a series of legislative innovations.

The first Customs for manoeuvreing sheep was instituted in Apulia in 1446. A census was completed with the *Tabulae censuariae*, tables or registers where the lands reserved for grazing were registered. It is from this that the Tavoliera, the Great Apulian Plain, takes its name. It is a land that leaves a strange sensation. The population is concentrated in large rural centres while the immense stetches of country are immersed in a profound solitude. It is a strange Italy, turned in on itself, fatalistic and immortal.

The old usages of the great movements of the flocks were modified by the abrogation of centuries old laws in 1806. The cultivation of cereals advanced and Foggia become the region's great market and agricultural emporium. But no economic or social transformation could erase the impression of proud, archaic solitude that these lands leave. The Magna Catapana remains a mythological world of villages marshalled on the hills, of luxurient harvests and of fields of grain yellowed by the sun. Carts roll slowly bringing the peasants back from work on an Apulian afternoon unique in the transparency of the air, in the diffuse luminosity and in the concentration of melancholy.
Passing from the Daunia and Capitanata to the Plain one enounters a world much more immersed in modern reality.
The landscape becomes more rational: the great fields of grain display an obstinate order, the winding roads leaving the long straight ways describe a web of perfect design. The Great Plain is Apulia transformed into a flourishing granary just as the far-seeing Lenormant had hoped for in 1866. It is a region where a perfectly balanced agricultural-industrial equilibrium has been well understood. Social revolution made it possible to halt the exodus of immigrants and to exploit new crops (hemp, cotton and tobacco) along with the mineral resources of the neighbouring Capitanata.
The Apulia of the Great Plain is no longer the immobile and romantic country of the nineteenth century prints. It no longer offers

material for fashionable imagery: the black figures of women; the sad profiles of lonely men; a sun that lashes the flocks of sheep; the dizzying sequence of dry wells in the droughts of high summer. Now the region flourishes with commerce and work, an exuberence of being busy. Foggia is the great commercial centre and communications junction.
A city of jealous beauty whose Cathedral happily combines Baroque and mediaeval forms. It is a city that lives by the complex texture of its commerce.
To the North is San Severo, the second great centre in the province where increasing economic development is linked with the cultivation of grapes and olives, with tourism and with industrial growth. A zone throbbing with activity, where the rhythm of life contrasts with certain traditional moments. The blinding luminosity of the white houses in the country evokes the purity of an archaic peasant world. Little by little as we advance towards the Gargano, there appear sharp mountain silhouettes of an almost sorrowful solemnity.
Monte Calvo's hump back interrupts the undulating plain adding a vigorous note to lands which, after reclamation, appear to be among the most intensely cultivated and the most fertile of the South.
Towns, hamlets and villages each have a very individual character. Apricena which hangs over the plain perched on a step 500 metres high; Sannicandro Garganico is a stoney landscape of surprising beauty where the spectacle of the Pozzatina, one of Italy's

greatest dolmens astonishes; San Marco in Lamis, a stop on the spiritual pilgrimage with its Good Friday procession; and San Giovanni Rotondo, the village gathered around the memory of its Capuchine convent.
The Northern coast is broken by the fine lakes of Lesina and Varano, an unexpected lagoon full of enchantment with the black dots of fisherman's boats plowing through the blue. And finally one arrives at the Gargano, the ravishing pearl of Apulia.
The promontory of the Gargano seems an escarpment that plunges down from the solitudes of the Capitanata. It is a sort of «island» of spectacular beauty which makes indentations in the low lying Adriatic coastline with its precipices and frames the Umbrian Forest in its heartland. The glacis of the Gargano peninsula is the «spur» of Italy. Its outlines begin at the height of Rodi Garganico. It continues towards Peschici and Vieste in a scenario of placid, tranquil inlets crowned with olive, pine, laurel and citrus fruit trees. Here too one is astonished by the incredibly stoney quality of the Gargano. It is a landscape of Dantesque variety where there are depths, grottos and unexplored chasms. The most extraordinary vision opens up between Peschici and Vieste: almost inconceivable for someone who has never seen it. A marvel of nature that leaves one breathless; it rises on a rocky promentory, a dizzying terrace with tall walls towards the sea and a gentle slope to the West where lies the fertile plain of the Padula.
Manacore is a bay dotted about with rocky

crags. It is a picturesque landscape with a limpid and transparent sea. The mystery of savage, blue-green caverns evoke legends of the Sirens, of Cyclops and of Ulysses. It is a sea behind whose rocks one sees mythical Ulyssian figures come ashore to set off on some arcane adventure. A people of poetic ghosts hang about those crags intent on making perennially suggestive gestures. Breaking up flints, collecting shellfish for sustenance, they repeat with a studied slowness the movements of a forgotten eternity.

The Gargano has reached us intact. It has succeeded in preserving itself from waves of speculation and noisy tourism. Its millenial motivations are still there. Its luminous coasts, its grottos charged with echoes and inlaid with azzure shadows. The sharp, heavy smell of pine trees.

Vieste is the easternmost centre of the Gargano. Its oldest and most evocative nucleus rises on the high and rocky point of San Francesco. All Apulia is represented here. The coast with its pines that almost dip their fronds into the limpid waters; the beaches and the crags that give way to sandy bights and inlets; ancient olive and almond groves and vineyards with all the perfumed variety of the Mediterranean scrub land. And here, too, are spiritual emotions in the basilicas and small rocky churches and in that enchantment that, with the ring of a prayer to Creation, takes hold of us before such a gilded and generous Mediterranean. Infinitely suggestive landscapes succeed one another: the bay of

San Felice where the « arcatello », a steep arch opened in the heart of the rocks, frames outcroppings in the sea; the bays of Campi, Portogreco, Pugnochiuso, Vignanotica; the grottos of the Smugglers, the Bottomless and the Two Eyes; and the grottos of the Two Doves, of the Marble, of the Sirens and of the Rooms. Everywhere one is struck by the chiseled composition of sunny whiteness; of forests with intense green splotches; and of the sculptured grottos surprisingly and prodigiously dappled in light and colour.

And in the heart of this enchantment lies the Foresta Umbra, a strip of ancient landscapes untouched by the devastation of mass civilization. A unique forest. An astonishing creation with brush strokes of the vivid blue sky that contemplates a panorama of beech, maple, hornbeam, turkey oak, oak lime, ilex, and pine trees. In the heart of it spreads a mysterious and diffuse light that has something of a church's astral penombre, the organ's magic sounds, yet at the same time is completely different from the arcane light of Northern forests populated with gnomes and elves. Perhaps there still moves here the ghost of Frederick II, a son of the North who came to hunt in this forest and who felt himself transported by a sort of drunkenness after having been kissed by the great blue skies and the sun of the South.

And twelve miles from the Gargano's nearest coast lie those golden fragments cast from the sky that are the Tremiti or Diomed islands. Their name alone makes one think. Does Tremiti come from *Tremetus* or from

Trimerus or *Trimerum* meaning trembling? Perhaps it recalls the rumble of ancient earthquakes that terrorized the islanders. Some seven hundred and fifty acres containing the sames of San Domino, San Nicola, Capraia, Cretaccio. They are shrouded in the legends of Diomede, king of Argus and Etolia, one of the noble heroes of the Trojan war, faithful companion of Ulysses. The Diomedian birds of the Albatross family, celebrated by Baudelaire, live along the Tremiti reefs. They have a particular nocturnal song, sad and anguished like the cry of one lost.

Legend has it that they were the most faithful warriors of the Argolid king and that the pity of the gods transformed them into birds so that they might weep eternally over the tomb of their glorious hero.

At San Nicola, a smooth and proud island, there is a tower. Charles II d'Anjou wanted a fortress built as a defense against Saracens and pirates. In this island the centuries of the Middle Ages are rich in tales of convents preyed upon: massacres of friars, ferocious Saracens, menacing fleets, burnings and mourning. Then in 1783 the Bourbon king transformed these islands into a penal colony. The misery of fishermen and peasants struggling for their meagre sustenance from the bowels of the sea and from the burned out earth met the misery of the convicts. Now there are no longer any convicts. The Tremiti attract only a vanguard of tourism hoping to pass a healthy holiday in contact with nature. Ferdinando Gregorovius wrote in his *Voyage in Italy:* «From the mountains of Apulia a long chain of hills stretches in a south-easterly direction towards the Terra di Bari and turning by Altamura and Gravina extends almost to the first heights that close the gulf of Taranto. These hills are the Murgia. They run along the border of the Basilicata, forming a mountainous land of uniform outline: monotonous, deserted and uncultivated; in part covered with oak wood and in part are of trees of brush. The slopes, however, offer excellent pasturage and here since time immemorial shepherds and hunters have gathered. The chain lies parallel to the sea, only about a mile distant from it». Even today it would be difficult to give such an exact aesthetic appreciation of the Apulian landscape. The Murgia is an intense universe of elementary contrasts: stone and grass, tree and rock, classical solemnity and modern torment.

The immense expanses of the Murgia are pervaded by a solitude that seems both mysterious and ancient. Burned lands extend with endless olive groves that become confused with oak woods. Almond plantations contrast with grey karst quarries in a singular symmetry: the quarries become great gardens as the meadows and the rock rhythmically alternate. And the sea should be taken into account: it is an integral part of the Murgia. It makes up the continual background, the component of human suffering. Apulia is the region of fishermen and peasants par excellence. Living from the sea and from the earth has created in it a different equilibrium. One is drawn to it by the spectacle of the handsome sea side towns built next to one another. This realistic equilibrium is to be found everywhere between nature and society, between marine and terrestrial resources, between the remote urban tendencies of the villages and the adventurous new initiatives of human groups. This is a land of those who build their own destiny with boats and with the bulldozer, with the fish net and with the plow. An «ant-like» people as that great student of the South, Tommaso Fiore, called them.

And here we are come into the tourist capital of these hills: the Murgia of the *trulli* as seen from Alberobello, the world's most typical village. It has been designed entirely by the singular architecture of the *trulli*. The Monti and Aia Piccola monumental zone boasts 1070 trulli scattered in picturesque disorder along the slopes of the hill. The largest, the *Trullo Sovrano* in the Piazza Sacramento, even has two stories. *Trulli* are very ancient constructions, born from materials of the past. The limestone strata or slabs make tiles laid without cement or binding agent to build these curious quadrangular huts. These shrink to a kind of pointed cupola culminating in a white pinnacle. Dwellings of a fairy tale realm, rich in suggestion: inimitable. The *trulli* derive from the Greek *tholos*. They have a profoundly magical and esoteric substratum. In reality they are neither dwellings nor monuments, but rather myths, symbols in stone. And in the stoney spirals there is depicted a graphic, enigmatic symbolism requiring contemplation and solution. These constructions may not even be antique, but the traditions that have generated them are extremely remote. And in splendid fashion they are inscribed in that rolling red earth plateau thick with low vines, green from the ilex groves and the carob scrub and edged by the interminable lines of little dry stone walls. Once upon a time the single room *trulli* were spread over the fields as sheds for agricultural implements. But then the rich land that was primitive Apulia became impoverished and the farmer himself came to live where once he had deposited his tools. The *trulli* became «shrines» which even the most distracted tourist dares not desecrate. These timeless islands are a Greek myth that lives in the luminous caress of the Murgia sun. Rich in the traditions that ennoble them, the *trulli* overlook the entire range of the landscape with the grace of grapes thickly clustered in a great bunch. The very landscape itself is unique and unrepeatable. It might ressemble the Carso at first sight, but it also has that outline and the meridianal softness of the English countryside.

The perfect amalgam of bleak nature and green shrubery, of restlessness and a cosmic Olympian serenity is created by the splendour of the great Mediterranean sky.

In this region, one should not miss a visit to the grottos of Castellana, the most spectacular geological complex in Italy. By a stairway of 110 steps one descends to the bottom of the Grava chasm where a labyrinth of glittering stalagmites leads into the grotto's entrance. The Caverna Bianca has been called «the most beautiful cave in the world».

And now the enchantment of Locorotondo and the Selva di Fasano awaits us. An enchanting terrace where the sea winds and those from the plateau mingle Cisternino with its vision of the East in houses white under the sun and the sweet gravity of the Romanesque church of San Nicola.

Now let's go towards Bari: crossing this land of little colour, so similar to other lands as to become confused in the midst of a remote timeless universe. History has left these places intact. Wars, economic changes and migrations; Levantine influences and the kingdom of Naples; the arrival of the «Piemontese» and the Kingdom of Italy; the great flight from the South and neo-capitalism; boom and impoverishment all passed over these lands like the sea over polished pebbles on the beach. Touching them, lapping over them, kissing them, but never digging them up or moving them. The appearance of stone and air, of sun and grass has remained the same: magnificent and immortal, unchanged through the centuries. To go to Bari from the Murgia, you need not follow the coast road alone nor only the Murgiana road. You can weave them together enjoying both the variety of the coast and the beauty of the hinterland on a route between bell towers, portals, rose windows and town squares. From Martina Franca and Cisterino we head along the road for Brindisi to discover ancient Ostuni, situated on three hills

that dominate a vast agricultural area of olive groves and vineyards. Returning along the coast towards Bari one comes across Monopoli, a city whose modernism reflects the vitality of Apulia today while its sparkling mediaeval nucleus overlooks the sea. Even Polignano a Mare looking over the edge of a cliff more than twenty metres high with immense grottos at its base, suggests a mediaeval village.

Beyond Bari to the West along the coast, Giovinazzo offers one of the best examples of the Apulian Romanesque cathedral. Molfetta has charming corners and unites the agitated quality of the modern city with the ancient placidity of a fishing village.

Strolling through the aisles of San Corrado, the largest of the Apulian Romanesque churches, one senses that aura of religious devotion that explains why the Crusaders chose to leave from here on their adventures. After Bisceglie and Trani, History comes forth to meet us. First the theater of the famous challenge the Barletta plain. Here in 1503 thirteen Italian champions, led by Ettore Fieramosca met and defeated the French champions, maintaining the symbol of national independence through dark days. And coming back to the country near where the Ofanto flows one encounters the clangor of horns and the sound of kettle drums of antiquity's most romantic battle: Cannae where Hannibal made the might of Rome tremble. The wind of the centuries blows over the vast burial ground cowering at the foot of the hill. For a long time it was thought to contain the tombs

of those fallen in the battle fought in 216 B.C. Instead it proves to be of a more recent epoch, of around the year 1000 and subesquently destroyed by the victorious Normans. Wandering through this majestic country, one reflects on the dizzying passage of time and on the transitoriness of human civilization. But if the hills and lands evoke an archaic and mythical Apulia, the cities instead mirror the world in a state of the greatest evolution. Bari has become an extraordinary centre of attraction with its inhabitants, highly active, punctual and faithful to schedules, celebrated as the «Milanese of the South». The city's valued realities are many: for the opening of the Fiera del Levante trade fair Italy's Prime Ministers traditionally speak on the state of the economy. The fair continues the great tradition of Apulia as a bridge to the East and its fabulous commerce. The Laterza publishing house has been synonymous with Italy's intellectual culture for a century. The university is one of the best in the country, with tens of thousands of students and several teaching chairs of extraordinary prestige. *La Gazzetta del Mezzogiorno* is a newspaper that has continued to grow in livelieness and authority, becoming among the best prepared and most committed in the civic sphere in Italy. Then there are the refined artistic manifestations of the Maggio.

I cannot help admiring the splendour of Brindisi's Aragonese Castle. Brindisi was the beautiful, true, principal port of the Empire looking to the East and became the springboard for armies and pilgrims heading towards the Holy Land. Here passed mercenaries, slaves, beautiful women and merchants. It is a land that has lived through all civilizations: the post-Roman, the Norman, the Aragonese, the Swabian and Saracen. Frederick II loved it passionately and called it with filial love: *Filia solis, ave, nostro gratissima cordi.* He understood it to be the cross roads of the then known universe. And on the map of Rainolfo Hyggeden of 1360 one reads: «Apulia whose metropolis is Brindisi. From here there are ships for the Holy Land». Taranto, the land of admirals and port captains. But its high noon was Baudelaire's exquisite hour when the colours in the sky, between two seas, have no equal in Europe. Lecce is a city of great migrations where Albanians, Greeks, Jews, Genoese and Florentines passed. Its building is entirely made of courtyards: small squares with a single access to the street, surrounded by typical two storey houses and a dizzy display of external staircases and balconies. Entire worlds pass in its bewildering architecture.

The Mesagnese courtyard was occupied by the Albanian colony while the Ragusan from Dalmatia practised money lending in the courtyard of the Campanella. Ever since then in these lands Ragusan is synonymous with usurer. Lecce is «a city closed within its own beauty» (Edgardo Bartoli). It is a sort of Apulia within Apulia, mysterious and insinuating.

Finally we descend to the extreme South, from Lecce to Maglie to Tricase to Santa Maria di Leuca; from Gallipoli to Copertino right in the Salentine peninsula.

An Ionian itinerary of the most fascinating and once again we feel that magical mixture of the archaic and the modern, of wild nature and of man's presence that is the splendour of Apulia. The land is still as very ancient as when the Greeks appeared here, but it is also resonant with work and activity. It is alive, pulsing with an inexhaustable throbbing. Along all the coast, towards an Otranto still redolent of the great Saracen massacre, one hears the suggestive evocations of the seas: the wild Adriatic, the Ionian and the Mediterranean, cradles of civilizations. And finally one is immersed in the poetry of the remote *Iapigium Promontorium* of ancient centuries. Capo Santa Maria di Leuca is the extreme southern point of the boot where the memory of past adventures lives in the sanctuary *The Finibus Terrae,* at the end of the world which was the goal of pilgrimages. Santa Maria di Leuca, Apulia's extreme archaic paradise. The writer who has best understood the riches of this land, Giuseppe Cassieri has said: here Italy ends. Or does it begin here? From the night of the millennia the boundless mystery of an eternal Apulia brings here, in the presence of its seas and plains, an inexhaustable life force.

Guido Gerosa

THE COASTS

Apulia has 800 kilometeres of coast line. This is not just a geographical fact: it is the sign of a destiny. A place of embarkation and debarcation for centuries, Apulia is above all land of the sea even if a Mysterious Fascination wafts from its occult lands. Over the centuries the Apulians have built their economic and cultural identity on the sea. The *Fiera del Levante* has a caravelle for its symbol, but other symbols could be the Crusader ships that left for the conquest of the East. The privileged bridge between the peninsula, the Dalmatian coast and Greece, Apulia has always built its reality on the sea. The coast has a splendour that De Biasi's magic photographs have captured in the pure state. But they show the inexhaustable wealth of port towns as well. Thus an extraordinary communications network intertwines in the heart of the Mediterranean which, although in the uproar of crisis, is again a sea extraordinarily rich in life and history. This sea represents an economic reality of the first order: the Apulian coastal system is based almost entirely on five major ports (Taranto, Brindisi, Bari, Manfredonia and Barletta). The other ports (Gallipoli, Monopoli, Otranto, Trani, Molfetta and the Tremiti islands) handle less than 500,000 tons of merchandise per year. Almost all traffic (74%) in the area of the five major ports is handled by the port of Taranto thanks to the presence there of Italsider. But now let's leave aside the economic reality and glance at the pure beauty of these coasts, among the most suggestive in Italy.

Pugnochiuso, brought to an intense life by the Eni works, charms with the supreme beauty of colour making it the pearl of the Gargano. The rocks twist into strange forms, almost like immense tortoises, which are reflected in the intensely blue sea. On their tops, in the midst of a crown of stones, the intense green of pine trees stands out. The handsome Hotel del Faro climbs the hill in big steps conjuring up an Andalusian dream. Its night lights animate a phantasmagoria worthy of a Fellini film. Before reaching Mattinata, coming down from Pugnochiuso, the fated bay of Le Zagare opens up, drenched in odours and perfumes like its name. Here, too, the reefs seem to imitate unreal sculpture and one is surprised by the immaculate luminosity of the waters. The Hotel delle Zagare, with its oriental accents and its dazzling whiteness, overlooks a scene of reefs of an extravagant architecture, almost the work of a great creator in a whimsical mood. At Vieste the coast extends for thirty jagged kilometres in a series of glimpses of fantastic beauty. The mediaeval town of Vieste is a fantasy from a tale of chivalry. Almost a rock in the rock, it rises majestically between the sea and the sky. And yet these coasts, so silent and intact, were the theatre, in past centuries, of frightening encounters. A stone placed next to the entrance of a fashionable locale recalls, sending a shiver up the tourist's spine, that it was on this spot in 1554 that 5,000 Viestani were decapitated by the Saracen pirate Dragut. The great attraction of Vieste is the Pizzomunno, a gigantic

monolith twenty metres tall. It appears to have detached itself from the great rocky mass of the precipitous cliffs. It is also linked to a tender legend. Cristalda, daughter of a goddess, fell in love with a humble lad from Vieste. She resorted to the goddess who struck poor Pizzomunno transforming him into a gigantic rock. Thus she took the loved one from her, but gave him immortality in the sea. And once every one hundred years, Pizzomunno returns as a youth and embraces his loved one in the night when all the waves glisten tenderly. The Tremiti islands were long a place of deportation, yet there are few islands anywhere in the world that equal them in beauty. They are a hand full of splendid rocks, coasts and bays lying some thirty kilometres from the spur of Gargano. Perhaps in antiquity they formed a single spit of land that closed off the Adriatic. Wild and savage, today they have been partly invaded by a wave of tourism. Still the island of San Nicola remains imposing in its proud solitude and on San Domino there rise the powerful walls of a monastery around which the history of this little archipelago revolved. The target of raids by fierce predators, the theatre of dissolute Boccaccian friars, this island has seen enough hisotry to fill a novel. These miraculous shores should be visited one by one. Trani, in the tranquil mirror of whose port churches, palaces and gardens are reflected while the slow and majestic flow of the waters recalls that it was here that the *Ordinamenta maris*, the most ancient

mediaeval maritime code, was born. And Molfetta is Apulia's most important centre for fishing with a fleet of over one hundred boats of which many are equipped for deep sea trawling. Its fish market is one of the most important in Italy. From the port one can enjoy the view of an intensely blue sea that deepens to purple on the horizon with strokes of deepest blue. One of the finest observation points for a panorama over the city is the old Duomo (XII-XIIIc.), one of the most majestic Apulian churches, rich in Lombard influences. The exterior is as simple as possible, yet pleasing and looks directly over the sea.
Art and natural beauty are here joined in a marvellous marriage.
From Bari to Polignano a Mare one enjoys an ever more varied and fantastic picture of coasts. They follow one another in such a wealth of landscapes as to excite the imagination of a great painter.
Curiously enough the beaches now seem to proliferate for the enjoyment of the tourist to these lands. On the coasts from Pugnochiuso to the Tremiti, from Gallipolli to Santa Maria di Leuca one sees few of those traditionally black female figures who bring the books of Verga or Capuana to mind. You are no longer pursued by the perennial vision of the ancient Apulian peasant woman, beautiful yet archaic, the creature of a millennial Greek world that proudly looks over the sea of the gods. Instead you see a modern girl who with her naked breasts melts in the sun, and whose bronzed body recalls an Hellenic goddess bearing all the unmistakeably sensual marks of the contemporary world. And you consider these provocative female forms with astonishment against a background of an eternal sea that is always renewing itself and in which the Greek dream of pure beauty has become a concrete yet magic reality.

4

5

7

11

12

14

15

16

18

HISTORY

In the surroundings of Molfetta great masses of stone formed like arches speak the language of ancient civilizations. The city of Egnazia was once great and propsperous on the Adriatic coasts. It stood on the border between Peucezia and Messapia. Now only a section of wall remains from the fourth or third century B. C. stretching out above a sea whose waves beat against its millennial stones. Its name recalls that Samnite soldier of fortune Gellio Egnazio who in 296 led a coalition of *quattuor gentes*, four nations – Samnites, Etruscans, Gauls and Umbrians – against Rome. The beautiful sculpture of a female head conserved at Taranto evokes the splendours of the Messapian girls. From Bari's museums comes the sound of trumpets, the trample of houses and the din of racing chariots. Meanwhile the traces of time have eaten like a moth into the togas and the faces of warriors and matrons in the statues of the Lecce museum. Lucera, with its arches, vaults and walls, recalls the raids of predatory Saracens who descended like sea hawks, devastating the country, massacring the men, taking off the boys and raping the women. At Troia history is written in those same strong structures of the cathedral with its profound Pisan influence and its Apulian grandeur. In the popular fantasy, Otranto still recalls the «great massacre». In 1480 the Turks of the Sultan Mohammed II burst into the cathedral and gave over to the sword the bishop and people who had sought sanctuary within. On the noutskirts of the city the Basilian monastery of Casole, one of the principal centres of mediaeval culture, was also destroyed. But there does survive an extraordinary document that the Saracen fury could not efface. The mosaic flooring of the Pantaleone presbytry is one of the most extraordinary figurative representations surviving from the Middle Ages with human beings, animals, and trees – a veritable triumph of nature and life. A tour of Apulia permits one to reconstruct, through cities and monuments, the traces of numerous civilizations that followed one another in this land so charged with history. Numerous vestiges of prehistory have come to light, testifying to the successive cultural phases in the development of a society over an arc of three thousand years. Between the Neolithic and the Bronze ages human settlements were numerous and particularly intense. From the most ancient times this region was the scene of great migrations which have left many traces between Italy and the Near East. The Romanelli Grotto (Diso) with its dazzling graffitti is a perfect stage in prehistory. In Apulia the Mesolithic age is called the Sipontinian era from the ancient city of Siponto near Manfredonia. In the Gargano, where the lower Paleolithic age is also present, it has left numerous traces. On the Foggia plain the villages present much evidence of the Neolithic, particularly of the inferior era. In that period the Apulia's ethnic groups were dedicated to agriculture, to cattle raising and to ceramic work. In the middle and superior phases of the Neolithic period Apulia fell under the influence of a Sicilian culture of about 4000 years earlier. This was the conclusive period of the preclassical Apulo-Materana civilization when Apulia frequently came into contact with the more northern civilizations of the Abruzzi and the Marches. Who were the ancient inhabitants of Apulia? Historians tell us that they came from Indo-European stock and that they arrived from Illyria or from the Aegean, particularly from Crete. The Greeks called them Iapygians and the Romans called them Apuli. The Iapygians spread over the Gargano and pushed on to Santa Maria di Leuca. They also came from northern Dalmatia and from the Epirus. These peoples migrated from the East to the West like the Arcadians, the Pelasgians, the Achaeans, the Trojans, the Cretans, and the Lydians and were led by civilizing heros, the founders of cities like Enotrio, Peucetius, Minos, Ulysses, Diomed, Aeneas, Antenor and Tyrrenus. The Iapygians were divided into the ethnic subgroups of the Daunians in the Capitanata and the Gargano; the Paucetians and the Pedicoli in the lands of Bari and the Murgia; and the Messapians in the Salentine. Between the nineteenth and the twelfth centuries before Christ there was at first an Aegean colonization followed by a Mycenean. The Iapygians put up a strong resistence to the Greeks who never succeeded in subjugating them. The Messapians instead came to terms with Greek influence accepted their alphabet. At the end of the eighth century the Greeks completed the penetration. Spartan colonies arrived from Laconia and founded Taranto,

Gallipoli and perhaps Otranto as well. The Messapian cities put up a strong resistence, but in the end were dominated by Taranto. Taranto in its turn demoralized by luxury and vice gave in to the new peoples, especially the Samnites in the fourth century. With the Samnite wars, Rome turned to the conquest of Apulia. At first defeated at Eraclea (280) and at Ascoli Satriano (279) by Pyrrus, king of Epirus, the Romans subdued Taranto in 272. On the plain of Canae, Hanibal won his memorable victory in 216 and the Apulian cities, with Taranto in the lead, rebelled against Rome. But Rome regaining the initiative, knew how to punish with severity. In 209 Taranto was reconquered and allowed to decay in favour of Brindisi the new gateway to the East.

Apulia become the centre of commerce with Greece, Asia Minor, Egypt and Syria. Brindisi was consacrated a municipality and its port, the most important in the peninsula, was linked with Rome by the majestic consular Appian and Trajanian roads.

In the Middle Ages, Apulia was the land of God. Its monasteries attracted pilgrims from all over Italy and from the East. The Gothic-Byzantine war (535-553) was a torment for the region. Then came the Longobard conquest. The Longobards occupied the Gargano and Canosa and completed the conquest of Brindisi (633) Taranto (675) and Bari (690). The Byzantines, left with a part of the Salentine, Otranto and Gallipoli, persevered in their resistence. But almost immediately afterwards the Muslims came sacking Brindisi (838) and Taranto (840). Saracen mercenaries enlisted by the Longobards took Bari (847) and reduced Apulia to misery. There followed a very long and tumultuous period with everyone fighting everyone else. In the meantime maritime activity developed along the coast while the monasteries flourished in the interior.

Then the Normans arrived. In 1043 William d'Hauteville assumed the title of Count of Apulia. In the period of the Crusades, the region was an obligatory point of passage for those hawks of the Faith who passed over into the Holy Land. As a result there was a flowering of commerce and business. But with the eclipse of the Swabian, the region slipped into decadence and was miserable under the Spanish domination (1503-1707). The coastal area became marsh land with malaria putting the population to flight. The Tavoliere plain was reduced to a labyrinth of sheep tracks. In 1799, during the Napoleonic era, Apulia was overrun by the legitimist troops of Cardinal Ruffo. But the brief French period (1805-1) with the reigns of Joseph Bonaparte and Gioacchino Murat, saw a revival and a promise of reform partly due to enlightened Apulians. It was a brief respite: the region once again fell prey to decadence and suffering. The Apulian middle classes participated with enthusiasm and committment in the Risorgimento. In the united life of the Italian State, Apulia again knew moments of difficulty and decline. But with the rise of industry and with the explosion of a new economic and cultural life, Apulia has taken up its historic role again as a driving force in the South, ever establishing new frontiers along which to advance.

28

29

31

32

36

37

39

40

42

43

45

46

RIMVS EPISCOPVS HCSECVNDA HICT RTIVS HICOMARTVS

TOR PORTARVM EVETODERISIVS HARVM BENEVENTANVS

ONVIALES PRSENAM ANNVLARVM AGENIOBI
ODEFATOR PORTA SÆNEAS PONTIFAT VERO MORE
BERATOR PENA DE RORIO ÆRA DNI HONORII PP CROANVS
MNVS GVI BIOLARGDSEN SEDI II ITEM PPLS ROLBER
LMVS SED SATOR BEEBILSSIT PONTIFLATVS DNI AETVENDA

FROM THE TRULLO TO THE SKYSCRAPER

The monuments of grey stone that rise in the heart of the country and that emerge, like a mystery, from the dense cactus, cry the lyric vitality of a land rich in ancient values and yet directed towards the future: from the *trullo* to the skyscaper. At dusk the walls of Massafra, furrowed by long flights of natural steps where the loop holes, open like penetrating eyes, are lit by suggestive purple reflections. The whole cliff near Massafra is perforated with grottos. These places still seem animated by the presence of those sainted hermits who in the Middle Ages retired to these solitudes to meditate and pray. The Baroque ramps that lead to the Sanctuary of the Madonna della Scala are an example of the happy fusion between natural art and landscape in an astonishing climate of ecstatic rapture.

The *trulli* of Martina Franca raise their grey cones surmounted by aery pinnacles to the clear sky. In Apulia the *trullo* represents a sort of landscape-state of the soul.

In substance it is an allegory of the house, a marvel of campactness and of classically rural proportions. Typical of the landscape of the whole Bassa Murgiana, the village world of the *trulli* extends from Alberobello to Noci, to Locorotondo, Putignano, Selva di Fasano, Ceglie Massapico and Cisternino with an extraordinary wealth of form and invention. With a single cell structure, the *trullo* is inspired by ancient architectonic models and takes its lines from the remote *tholos* tombs of Mycenae. There are many imitations in the Mediterranean area: *nuraghi* in Sardinia, *sesi*

on Pantelleria, *talayots* in the Balearics and *timboni* on Sybarus. Even contemporary examples faithfully imitate the millennial tradition. The blocks of stone are laid on one another on a square plan without cement. The circles above shrink until they form the vaults. The whitened and plastered external walls dazzle in contrast to the black tiles that cover the roof cone. Clean, white interiors have niches and beds dug out of the internal walls. The spherical, star-shaped or pine cone pinacles are fantastic. Once upon a time the black roofs were painted with whitewash figures of every sort (seals, monograms, religious and pagan, astrological and ornamental emblems) that served to invoke divine protection.

Were there nothing else in Apulia, Alberobello alone would be enough to represent the beauty and arcane mystery of an entire region. In this village, which traces its origins to an abbey of the sixth century, the *trulli* enliven the landscape with a marvellously poetic happiness. There are 1070 dwellings of typical rounded form crowned with the tall conical roof. When did the *trulli* spread throughout the Murgia? The oldest and most certainly dated is of 1559. But the greater part are more recent with their construction at the end of the eighteenth through to the end of the nineteenth centuries. Many of the *trulli* are continuous dwellings and house more than one family. The roof is, for the most part, used as storage space: a granary or a wood shed. Rising above all the others is the stupendous «sovereign *trullo*» 15 metres tall.

The suggestive church of Sant'Antonio fits into the same spirit of this landscape, imitating the daring fantasy of the *trulli* in its form. Throughout Apulia there is this remarkable synthesis of the archaic and the landscape, of the sea and the country, of art and nature. And everywhere, too, there is the blinding glare of whitewash.

But the whitest village of them all is Ostuni which extends its colour along the Murgia plateau in full view of the wild Adriatic. The profile of the old city is endlessly fascinating with its white houses and its sod earth of a dark green colour: with its strips of pink light and the sky of that soft Apulian blue that, in certain moments, seems as pale as a tear. The mediaeval nucleus of Ostuni is contained within the circle of old bastions where the crowded throng of houses seems to suggest a mythology of a land with profound ties to the past yet free. Stairways, terraces with gardens, blinding white wash the colour of milk. In the glimmer of evening when the lids of the sky are weighed down, Ostuni has the remote softness of an island lost in Aegean. In the heart of the Gargano spur, at Monte Sant'Angelo, picturesque stairs plunge to the bottom of a theatre of white houses. The village rises at 800 metres on the brow of the promontory. It spreads towards the Adriatic and is continually beaten by the wind. The clear sky illuminates a scene of ancient dreams. This is one of the most blessed places in Europe. Many saints will go up to this mountain – Bernard, Francis of Assisi, Thomas Aquinus, Catherine of Siena – and then popes, emperors and crusading knights. They were anxious to kneel in prayer in the magic grotto where one of the most famous sanctuaries of Christiantity arose, dedicated to the Archangel Michael.

Colours taken from the earth and sky enliven Locorotondo, possibly the most stupendous of Apulia's villages. Locorotondo has a completely unexpected aspect. Roofs, each illustrating its own suprising architecture, occult silences and the black of the sharp overhang, stand in contrast to the dazzling Mediterranean whiteness of the houses. The white walls recall Arab villages, although the style of steep roofs evokes the spirit of Nordic houses. This extreme variety in the landscape, this magic wand that captures waves of distant towers, confers on the Valle d'Itria town a completely inimitable character.

At Cesarea the embroidered patterns on the walls of houses and palaces seem a fine inlay of lace and needlework. In these parts one feels the sweetness of life and the soft despair of the Normans, as handsome as Northern gods, yet perennial exiles from their own land. The lament of king Frederick echoes between the orange walls of the Castel del Monte. This beautiful town was erected by the will of Frederick II between 1240 and 1250 on the Murgia heights. It enjoys a majestic vista from the Adriatic to the mountains of the Basilicata. The Emperor wanted to make it his hunting residence but life had fled from him before he could realize his dream. The castle, under that sky's enchantment, is one of the most beautiful constructions in Apulia and the masterpiece of Frederick's era. Even the cities participate in the purity of those landscapes. Taranto with the clear cut clarity of its buildings and with that omnipresent smell of the sea; Brindisi is walls and gardens; and Lecce with the festival of its Baroque animated by volutes, cherubs, carved blocks and festoons. A tidal wave of architectural fantasy that has crashed into originally sober structures. And in Bari, finally, the pulse of modern life triumphs: traffic, a heavy rhythm and skyscrapers. The futuristic point of arrival of a magic land where grains of african sand blow in a city of solid whiteness standing between the Nordic and the Mediterranean.

52

58

59

63

64

68

69

71

72

76

77

THE LANGUAGE OF THE STONES

Stone is the great protagonist of life in Apulia. The stones of the churches, of the palaces and of rocks that have their own language here; a voice that rises from the depths and expresses itself with mysterious echoes. That warm grey rock, the stone of ancient groaning, sings the memory of remote eras and perennial Mediterranean mythology. Authoritatively inscribed in a niche in Lecce is the outline of the winged lion of Saint Mark, symbol of peace and force. Ever for the Apulian fishermen and navigators, it is a millennial stone in a land which the Crusaders used as the jumping off place for their undertakings in the Holy Land.

At Trani a succession of picturesque white steps rises between the sea and the sky directly over the great theatre of the waves. The city that appears from afar is furrowed by cathedral shadows. Grand arches of daring shape emerge from the morning's clear surface and the language of the stones is coloured by a thousand unexpected echoes.

A little way from the city, with its face to the sea, stands Trani's Cathedral which, with the name of San Nicola Pellegrino, is one of the most beautiful monuments in Apulia. Erected between 1056 and 1186, it is composed of two superimposed churches. The entrances to the upper church open into a terrace reached by two staircases that are a hymn of clear and airy stone. The façade is slender, rising on a tall base. Low down, it is broken by a series of nine blind arches. These are the arches of an old door that was never completed. Here it is that ancient stone, the dream of a glorious past, triumphs. In the crypt a dense jungle of columns produces an intense effect of evocation.

Trani was the ancient Turenun or Tyrenum, a Iapygite city about which very little is known before the third and fourth centuries after Christ. In the ninth century the Saracens attacked and devastated nearby Canosa. Trani took in the refugees and, reinforced by the new population, became an important centre.

Touring Apulia one discovers caryatids drawn in stone, statues that are inserted into the scenic play of lively façades, capitals, volutes and ornamental motifs leading right up to the festive and lavish stones of Lecce's Baroque. At Martina Franca there are examples of great decorative wealth: heads of cherubs, warriors, horses and a fantasy of coats of arms.

A balcony in Turi glows in the preciousness of wrought iron with all the fascination of imagery and in the sinuous design of its railing with a variety of arches and friezes and the blaze of an escutcheon.

Here stone is converted into the elegance of architectonic lines and into the purity of the classical rhythms that pervade it.

At Galatone we come to the heart of Baroque Apulia where even the wind has a special tinkling sound. The buildings ave astonishing for the realth of ornamental motifs which culminate in wonderment. Stone here is «storied» and full of light with the representation of leaves, animals, tracery and with chasing and inlay to the point of affectation. The windows of the churches are lace work and yet are inserted between pilasters of a golden simplicity. Galatone's treasure is the Sanctuary of the Crocifisso della Pietà (1696-1710). This agricultural centre of the Salento has lived through many historic vicissitudes. It was fortified after the year 1000; it was sacked and devastated first by the Turks and then by the Venetians at the beginning of the fifteenth century. It has been the feudal possession of great families: the Falcone, the Sanseverino, the Del Balzo, the Castriota, the Spinelli and the Pignatelli. The Sanctuary of the Crocifisso della Pietà is among the most exciting works in all Apulia presenting a wealth of endless motifs. Freizes, niches, pediments and windows closed by pierced stone screens along with a Renaissance doorway. This itinerary through stone brings us to that prodigy of colour that is the Baroque of Lecce. Here the stone really shouts. It throbs with colours and life in an extraordinary way. There emanates from those churches the powerful gusts of religious spirit that is at the same time both secular and like the odyssey of a people that stretches out over the sea. The façade of the church of Santi Nicolò and Cataldo is one of most classical examples of Lecce's beauty and also the most important example of the Romanesque style in the Salento. It was founded by Tancred d'Hauteville in 1180 and represents a refined kaleidoscope of Byzantine, Muslim and proto-Gothic influences. The ornamental motifs are so agitated and animated that they give a sense of the sea's proximity and its presence in the world of Apulia.

Looking at these stones is like seeing the waves breaking from afar; seeing the salt air's inspiration; hearing the wave's breathlessness as a presentiment of the sea. It is a fabulous sensation like being seized by the double magical music of stone and of words. A poem of Borges comes to mind: « The sea is endless. Thus fish, green / Cosmic serpent that encloses / Green serpent and green sea, the earth / Like a circle ».

Cathedral rose windows have their own language. A great light comes from tracery as delicate as embroidery of Ostuni's rose window. And here is the eagle that, with its threatening outline, overshadows Gravina di Puglia's rose window. Trani's is a perfect circle, a severe relief that emerges from a sober façade of compact grey stone. The rose windows of Otranto, Troia and Ruvo di Puglia are extremely elegant. Troia's above all is an extremely refined arabesque with embroidery, tracery and exquisitely conceived chasing. The character of the Apulian people seems to come out of the stones of the statues in the old cathedrals. That proud aspect of the men, sweet in the women, goes back to the history of the earliest Italy. Stone faces of young maidens are fixed in a tender inquisitive smile. In certain reliefs there are Christs of a sevenly hieratic, Romanesque type: the limbs squared by the artist with a rough geometry; the praying and devout lined up with their eloquent silence in grave procession. The imposing statues, before which the boy from Gallipoli in the orange jersey remains enchanted, are a triumph of mature, thick, porous stone. The limbs sculpted with muscles tightly gathered ready for release. Even the reclining or seated creatures breath an intense vitality, a secret spring of life and passion.

And here again is Lecce with its intelligent scenic follies; with the twisted columns of its canopies that evoke Bernini's ghosts, with the simpler, more linear columns that evocatively frame windows through which trees and nature accompany the epic and lyric rhythm of the stone.

An intense symphony of greys, a language of profoundly rhythmic cadences, a limitless wealth of art and history.

The fullness of a dream that makes Apulia great becomes a reality in this language of stone.

87

88

90

91

93

94

95

97

98

99

100

101

102

103

104

MEN, WORK, FESTIVALS

There has been a radical transformation in Apulia in recent years. Industrialization has brought the ferment of a new world and the very quality of men has changed.

The populace of peasants, of fishermen and of seamen devoted to a trade and commerce directed towards the East has partly abandoned traditional agricultural activity and has dedicated itself with passion to the new industrial structure which government agencies and private investors have bequeathed to the region. Agriculture itself has become rational and offers earnings superior to those of the past. Sheep breeding is in decline even in the areas like the Tavoliere plain where it was practised following ancient traditions.

The flowering of the region has been made possible by public works of great importance like the Apulian Acqueduct which has brought water everywhere. From Margherita di Savoia to Taranto, from Lecce to Foggia one can instantly perceive the vitality, the fever of work that has invaded the new Apulia. Agricultural production is rich with the cultivation of sugar beets, linen, tobacco, fruit, quinces, dried figs and pears; and vegetables like artichokes, cabbages, cauliflower and musk melons. This imposing production permits a broad based exportation towards Northern Italy while feeding a prosperous industry of foodstuffs and its conservation that is at the very heart of Apulian industrial activity.

Mineral and energy resources in Apulia are scarce with the exception of bauxite in the Gargano and Salento, of bentonite in the Apennines and in the Tremiti islands and of marine salt in the vast salt pans of Margherita di Savoia.

The development in the Tavoliere plain of a centre near the banks of the Otranto, is linked to the presence of salt pans, been exploited in the Roman era as among the most important in Europe. More than five million quintals of salt a year or 70% of the total production of the government monopoly is produced in these extremely modern salt refineries for consumption, industry and for use among animals. A high speed cable car system connects the salt pans with the port of Barletta. Their waters are used partly in factories that produces bromides for industrial use and partly in a bathing establishment.

The impressive Taranto refinery and the immense iron works have given a powerful impulse to the growth of the region.

Among the primary industrial activities are the mechanical and electromechanical installations at Taranto, Bari, Brindisi, and Foggia which should be mentioned along with the chemical plants at Bari, Barletta and Brindisi; tobacco manufactory at Lecce; the manufactory of cellulose and paper at Foggia. Sea fishing molusc breeding and fish nurseries such as that practised in the lakes of Lesina, Varano and Salpi have a notable economic importance. Commerce has always been the soul of the region and the means for intensive exchange with other Italian regions and with countries of the Eastern Mediterranean. The living symbol of Apulian commerce is the Fiera del Levante trade fair instituted in 1930 at Bari. In recent years tourism has been developed in the Gargano (Vieste, Pugnochiuso). But despite promoting it and making it an important activity, the Apulians have carefully avoided allowing it to assume those destructive aspects of consumerism based on mass appeal.

What is the Apulian man like? We have seen him, even at his most mysterious, in the course of this exploration of the region. The Apulian has a strong willed and rigorous character, a polemical eloquence, yet a great open mindedness, a fertile intelligence, and a very vivid curiosity. His is a populace of highly evolved human beings, having a dynamic concept of life and, used to contact with other peoples since Antiquity. The Apulian's dominant characteristic is their religious anxiety. One need only think of the spirituality evoked at San Giovanni Rotondo by the still haunting, mystical presence of Padre Pio.

Thus festivals and traditions almost always have a religious frame of reference in Apulia. We have seen how there exists in truly spiritual itinerary for pilgrimages in the Gargano. There, indeed, one finds the most mystical place in Apulia: in a grotto where today the celebrated sanctuary of San Michele Arcangelo is to be found, the archangel appeared in the form of a man in 490 during the papacy of Gelasio I. The sanctuary rose on the site of this prodigy and became one of the major goals of pilgrimage in Western

Christendom. Pilgrims and Crusaders headed for the Holy Land would stop there. It became as famous as the Holy Sepulchre in Jerusalem or the tombs of the Holy Apostles in Rome or the shrine of Santiago di Compostella in Spain.

In 1807 sailors from Bari, seeing the Muslim threat to the city of Myra in Asia Minor, stole the remains of the Bishop Nicholas and brought them to Bari. From then on San Nicola was the patron of the city where, every year between May 7-8 there take place great festivities in his honour. A picturesque parade advances through the streets in the night amid the blaze of torches and lanterns bringing the Saint's statue to be deposited on the floating altar made on a fishing boat, symbol of the vessel that brought the saint's relics to Bari. After three days of festivity the faithful return home bringing the Santa Manna, a liquid believed to be distilled from the bones of Saint Nicholas.

The festivals of Apulia furnish endless material for sociological study. At Brindisi there is the «procession of the adorned horse» for Corpus Domini. This recalls the legend of Saint Louis IX the King of France who, returning from Jerusalem in 1252 was driven with his ship onto the coast by a great tidal wave... He was carrying the Eucharist with him aboard the ship. At Bari the «procession of the Mysteries» on Good Friday is suggestive, while at Taranto there is the classic procession of the *Perdune* (the pardoned) that recalls pilgrims going to Rome to ask forgiveness for their sins. The members of the confraternities parade two by two at an incredibly slow pace singing and wearing hoods with two eye holes giving them a mysterious and terrible appearance.

At Molfetta on September there is the feast of the Virgin of the Martyrs; at Bari the Ascension tide feast recalls the victory of the Venetian Doge Pietro Orseolo II over the Saracens. This is the equivalent of the famous Venetian feast of the Marriage of the Sea.

At Lecce the population participates in a religious festival with the making of the *Pupi*, splendid sacred images in papier mache for the Fiera that takes place between December 13-24. At Ostuni in the province of Brindisi the festival of the patron saint, Sant'Oronzo, is celebrated on August 26 with a beautiful parade on foot and on horesback of variously sparkling, scarlet vestments. Religion is permeated with the Middle Ages everywhere and also with Paganism. In several of the more mysterious Apulian villages self flagellation is still practised. Even that is a symbol of a thrust towards the eternal that still conserves all the signs of mystery, of fear and of the sublime.

111

112

116

117

119

121

123

124

125

126

127

128

129

130

134

135

137

138

139

143

144

unione
camere
commercio
PUGLIA

NATURE

Nature in Apulia is one of the happiest aesthetic moments in the Italian landscape. The reason it is less well known than certain parts of Campania or of the Sicilian sea, or even that celebrated parts of the Roman Campagna or the Tuscan hills is that because of its own reserve or because of its inhabitants tenacious modesty, the region was avoided by the great travellers, especially the foreigners who in the eighteenth and nineteenth centuries undertook the Grand Tour of Italy and left those descriptions that fill anthologies even today.

Apulia was less «celebrated». It is difficult to find famous pages that describe the intensely blue sea, the pearl grey enchantment of the olive groves, the bitterness of the mountain ranges, the scent of the orange blossoms, the «terribilità» of the processions, the slow transferral of the flocks from the hills to the sea. And yet the Apulian landscape is in itself a variety of prodigious beauty. It is a shame that it only attracts scientists anxious to describe the misery of its marsh land or the neglect of its governments. But perhaps this has served to save it from the agression of tourism.

Today fully appreciated, the Gargano seems one of the proudest Italian landscapes. The rocks have a precious grey subtlety and the beaches possess an immensity and the limitless fascination of an African shore. The sea is quiet and mysterious, echoing the song of ancient Mediterranean legends, the myths of Ulysses and the Sirens.

And the olive groves of the Salento breath the presence of time in an unmistakeable way. There is here the enchantment of a prodigious antiquity, a vast shadow of the past spreads through those aged hunch trees, in those fields of the low walls and in the white houses. There is a charge of the history of centuries which we can feel immediately almost as if it were music. At times there appear to be wells of stone that continue to be dug right down to the beginnings of time. Even the noise of the excavators or of the agricultural machinery seems to be transformed, in the solemnity of the plains, into a vast quiet, silence.

Low horizons full of colour and of the steely transparencies of autumn, purple clouds, the ordered song of the olive groves: this is the magic of the lake of Varano, especially at dusk. A grey that has the precious quality of mother of pearl. The ancient ghosts are present in the air having shaped the souls' eternal appearance.

Apulia is above all a feeling, a way of being, a landscape described as a state of the soul. Its stones, its waters have a sonority, a resonance that would be inconceiveable elsewhere. Emerson, who was a lover of nature, said that language is a fossil. In Apulia there never seems to be the gap between the word and the landscapes, between the visible and the musical. Looking at the lake of Lesina: the waters are so very still yet make one think of a mysterious magma, of a subterranean moving life. Finite and at the same time limitless: boundless like the poetry of Horace who as Borges says, still remains the most mysterious of poets because his verses make conclusions but never end and taken together seen to be disconnected.

The most complete sense of the Apulian's reality is provided by the visions of the Foresta Umbra at the heart of the Gargano. A magical space, populated by deer and other mythical animals where the lazy wind whistles through the branches as if it were a slow river bringing the distant northern air which enchanted the Emperor Frederick II who hoped to make his residence in this place. And yet that forest bears in itself all the symbols of Apulia's eternal mystery. A delicate dusk: eternal without before or after, the sweet season of myths. Light flees and plays hide and seek, hiding itself amid the trees. A mysterious harp gives off an invisible music, the gift of time. Animal shadows continually flee in this secret, grey and furtive realm of the shadow. Thus the Foresta Umbra, never sung by poets nor described by travellers, surprises us for the hidden quality of its beauty which has become a commonplace for prayer and magic.

One emerges from this immersion in the immense and unknowable and returns to the deep blue of the Gargano and the Tremiti islands. This is the ancient Greek sea of Poseidon and Homer. But «time and its wars», as Borges says in narrating Poseidon, «are taken away by the presence of God, while the sea remains its highest effigy». And then explains «There is not one thing in this world that is not mysterious, but mysteries are more evident in certain things than in

others. In the sea, in the colour yellow, in the eyes of the old and in music». Buffalos move silently in the bogs of Bitonto like a quiet, homely Vietnam. And one is struck everywhere in Apulia, in the Tremiti islands, on Gargano and on the plains, how these silhouettes of ancient animals appear, only to quickly vanish in the darkness. The same vivid light of the sky is sucked away by the infinite darkness. It is as if the Mediterranean glare and luminosity turned in on themselves and wrapped themselves in the mystery and ambiguity characteristic of the universe. Light is always spreading over the beaches and in the forests, in the villages and over the white houses perched in the hills, like a light silvery liquid, a scintilating Christmas rain. Perhaps this explains yet once again why foreign travellers avoided Apulia. Here the most profound and secret sensation of primitive Italy are closed up: the incorrupt nobility of the Messapians, the Peucetians and the Iapygians: the undiluted strength of lost peoples. This land become the Mediterranean's little Atlantis, submerged in the burning shadows of its great history; devastated, burdened and buried by Byzantines, Saracens, Franks, Longobards, Swabians, Angevins, Normans and Italians yet always remaining whole like the sleeping beauty. A land that is alive, sensitive and piercing like a wound. Its nature is silent and wild as in the grottos of Castellana, all stalagtites and stalagmites, vivid red and glowing with arcane presences.
Then the sea reappears, a revelation, the theophany of Apulia. Rocks permeated by a marine luminosity in the Bay of the Zagare; flights of festive birds rising up at Vieste; the firey chariot of the gods fleeing into the great sunset behind the ball of the sun.
In the dark the noises of the past return: the hoes that dig into the rocky earth; Crusader ships that set sail for the Holy Land; an incessant music of strance light noises; thin faces that twitch; the heat of the earth that burns above, within and around the villages. A world that is often of an impetuous burning but that still conserves the occult presence of the unknown god. A nature that is so beautiful that it cannot even be described. «Every memorable man», the beloved Borges says «runs the risk of being shortchanged by anecdotes». But Apulia steadfastly refuses to be reduced to an anecdote. It is itself and that is enough. It fills eyes and heart leaving you without words. It is absolute and imperious. Only that inexpressible, infinite essence of ambiguity and mystery which gives imagery to civilization can gather and capture the fleeting essence forever.

151

160

161

165

166

168

169

INDEX OF PLACES

Jacket:
Modern *trulli* at Alberobello.

Back jacket:
Baia delle Zagare.

Endpapers:
Brindisi, detail of the façade of the church of Santa Maria del Casale.

Facing the frontispiece:
Gargano, Baia delle Zagare.

The Coasts

History

From the *trullo* to the skyscraper

The language of the stones

The photographs in this volume were taken with a Contax RTS2 and 139 Quartz using the following Zeiss lenses: 18 mm f. 4; 35 mm f. 2,8; 60 mm f. 2,8; 100 mm f. 2; 300 mm f. 4; and many others with a Vivitar Zoom 70-210 f. 3,5.
All the photographs were taken in natural light without flash or other artificial illumination using Ektachrome Professional film for daylight photography.

Printed by Grafiche Lema of Maniago/Pordenone/Italy
in July 1986

Editorial consulting:
PRC, Rome

Consultant for photolithography and printing:
Enrico Mazzoli

Photolithography:
Graphicolor/Milano

—